To my dear friend

_____

_____

I Call Thee Friend

A Keepsake for My Bridal Attendant

ARLENE HAMILTON STEWART

Andrews and McMeel
A Universal Press Syndicate Company
Kansas City

Introduction

When a man and a woman decide to marry, part of the thrill is announcing the news to their friends and family. No sooner are the words out than cries of delight and congratulations fill the air, and tears of joy barely dry before the planning begins. At this wonderful time in a woman's life, emotions are heightened, friendships are deepened. And in a ritual that is as old as time itself, the bride draws close friends closer, asking them to share her joy by agreeing to be her bridal attendants.

Throughout the ages, women have provided help and emotional support for each other. In ancient Greek ceremonies, the bride was accompanied to the nuptials by an honor guard of older married women, who symbolized the wisdom of wedded life. During the days of brides-by-capture, when women were abducted from their tribes by grooms on horseback, young maidens banded together to protect their friends. Later, as marriage became a social institution, these

early guards evolved into a more ceremonial, though no less affectionate, presence—the bridal attendants.

To a Victorian bride, a wedding was the emotional highlight of her life. She and her bridesmaids drew close, spending many pleasant hours together stitching up trousseaux, planning showers and teas, rushing off to fittings and prenuptial parties. And today, when the modern bride needs advice or a helping hand, moral support, or just a good friend to have a cup of tea with at the end of the day, she will turn to her bridesmaids.

Planning a wedding can be an exciting and exhausting undertaking. But every moment of it is made brighter and sweeter by the special bond between the bride and her bridal attendants and the growth of the friendship between them as one of them prepares for married life.

Each friend

represents a world in us,

a world possibly

not born until they arrive,

and it is only

by this meeting that a new

world is born.

ANAIS NIN

• Asking a Loving Favor •

One of the greatest compliments a woman can receive is to be asked to be in her friend's wedding. "A happy bridesmaid makes a happy bride," observed Alfred, Lord Tennyson a century ago. For most women, their wedding is the most important milestone in their lives. Whether she opts for a simple ceremony in a judge's chambers or a lavish country club celebration, from the moment the bride-to-be announces her great news until she leaves on her honeymoon, her days will be filled with more planning and scheduling, details, and shopping than she can imagine. Throughout

this flurry of activity will be many moments of gaiety and excitement. Having special friends to share them makes it all the more wonderful.

The prospective bride has of course given lots of thought to her wedding party. Sisters, cousins, close friends—she would like to include everyone. All she needs to remember is that this is her wedding—she may select a maid of honor, a matron of honor, as many bridesmaids as she wishes, or simply waltz down the aisle behind a flotilla of beaming flower girls. There is no right and wrong this day, only what makes her experience a richer and happier one.

If you have been chosen to be a bridal attendant, yours is a happy task. By asking you to be in her wedding party, the bride-to-be has confirmed her deep affection for you. Far more than a gesture, this pact between you two is an echo of the sentiment women have shared for generations as they guide each other down destiny's path. Throughout the parties, planning sessions, lunches, fittings, and rehearsals, the bridal attendant is there for her friend. And on the wedding day itself, the bridesmaid, through the radiance and beauty of her own countenance, conveys the profound feeling she holds for the bride.

How does the prospective bride ask for a favor this wonderful? Perhaps, like many tightly woven friendships, yours is one that needs no formal words. An afternoon tea with pretty cakes or a breakfast party featuring foods you both love would provide a charming informal setting. Small wedding charms attached to handwritten notes can give quiet voice to the bride's request.

· A Helping Hand ·

$\mathcal{T}$he announcement is made and the date is set. Suddenly there seem to be so many things to do— guest lists, invitations, seating plans, wedding favors, menus, flowers, showers. Besides her groom, the bride has a host of allies in this wonderful experience—her good friends in the bridal party. Part therapists, part advisers, they know intuitively how to take some of the pressure off the bride, especially by helping her get organized— after all, if love is the heart of all weddings, then planning is the backbone. Fortunately, there are lots of ways to make these tasks

more pleasurable, starting with sending out the wedding invitations. Traditionally, bridal attendants are called upon to help out; if it is a large wedding, this will be a big job. But the bride and her attendants can make this into a festive occasion—first working side by side, then relaxing afterward with a luxurious lunch or tea. In a quiet spot and with beautiful inks and fountain pens, arrange yourselves around a large writing surface. Remember, the invitation is the guests' first taste of the tone and tenor of the wedding. Use your best hand and address each envelope clearly, tucking in personal notes from the bride when appropriate. A supply of special-issue stamps from the post office, perhaps engraved with a state flower or bird, will make the envelopes even prettier.

You may want to think ahead and find a unique way to organize the responses that will be arriving in a few weeks' time. A special basket or fabric-covered box for just this purpose would make a charming gift to the bride-to-be. Present it to your friend at tea, along with the offer to help compile the final guest list and seating plan right before the wedding.

During the busy afternoon, talk may turn to the topic of bridal fashions, and as the many details are discussed, you embark upon another exciting element to which the bridesmaid can give so much. A bride is always appreciative of her friends' counsel, and there is no time like a wedding for getting true thoughts on what to wear, what looks best. Sipping tea, or perhaps late-afternoon champagne, you talk freely about dreams, about the wedding outfit the bride has always seen herself wearing, the mood she wants to set for her wedding. Every detail fascinates, from length of veils to color of shoes. Suggestions and ideas, some serious, some

outrageous, may fly through the air. But soon the moment arrives when ideas are put into reality. Some brides love to pour over every bridal magazine available. Others have always had an inner vision of what is right for them. Many brides and bridal attendants plan a shopping strategy. In search of the "right thing," they may visit big shops and small boutiques, wedding designers, or favorite vintage clothing stores. Colors, fabrics, laces, trains—it may seem like too much, until that magic moment when the bride appears in something so exquisite that you know instantly it is the perfect choice, the only choice. Soon the quest begins for the shoes, gloves, jewelry, even flowers, but now you have completed a major accomplishment.

Another lovely piece of the wedding mosaic for you to share with the bride is choosing ensembles for the bridal party. For centuries, bridesmaids were enrobed in wedding finery every bit as grand as the bride's. In fact, it was a custom up until the late nineteenth century for bridesmaids to dress in gowns and veils identical to that of the bride! A long-held superstition maintained that at any wedding evil spirits would be lurking

about, jealous of the bride's good fortune. To confuse these malevolent spirits, brides and bridesmaids dressed alike. Later, as brides realized this was nothing more than a superstition, they felt confident about dressing differently from their attendants. Today, bridesmaids often all wear the same style dress as one another, usually in a rainbow of pastels—soft lilacs, pale blues, greens, pinks—or perhaps in deeper jewel tones, in sophisticated black, or even in white. But this custom is changing, too. Bridesmaids are not always all of the same age, size, and stature. It is not unusual to include very young friends, or even children from previous marriages, as bridesmaids, especially when there is more than one candidate for flower girl. Having older friends serve as attendants is a popular new custom, particularly in light of the number of second marriages and the deep friendships that are often formed between professional women.

Whatever styles and colors the bride and her bridesmaids select, the act of finding them together is another important link in the chain of collaboration between friends that just keeps growing stronger.

• Showers of Friendship •

*J*ust as it is a centuries-old custom for friends of the bride to host a shower for her, it has long been a tradition for the bride to give a party or "tea" for her bridal attendants to thank them for all the contributions they have made to her happiness. This is a small, intimate party usually held in the weeks just before the wedding. It is at this Bridesmaids' Tea that many brides give each member of their wedding party a special present. It is a lovely idea to mark this occasion with a small memento— potpourri in lace sachets, silk handkerchieves, perfume bottles, silver combs and brushes, or tussie-mussies of sweetheart roses.

The tea can be a brunch held at a favorite bistro, a picnic at a fabulous garden. Or it needn't be a tea at all, but a glamorous "girls only" dinner party where everyone dresses up and toasts to the future with fine wines and witty sayings. In Great-Grandmother's day, a white frosted cake would sit upon a pedestal awaiting the dessert course; baked inside would be silver charms that symbolized marriage—knots, bows, hearts, and, for the one lucky person in whose slice it appeared, a ring that "guaranteed" that she would be the next to marry. Of course, the bride knew where the best charms were located and would cut the cake accordingly. This sweet custom is as much fun now as then.

The Bride's Shower held in the bride's honor is usually given by members of her wedding party. Legend has it that centuries ago, the parents of a young Dutch maiden denied her both a dowry and permission to marry a poor cobbler. Seeing her misery, her female friends "showered" her with household goods so that she could marry the man she loved. Today's shower is a re-creation of that loving act, a time-honored way of helping a couple set up home and become members of the larger community. Often it has a specific theme: a linen shower, lingerie shower, kitchen or garden shower. While the days of the deluge of the toaster seem to be gone, it is always wise to ask the bride in advance what the couple really needs. Candor at this point is not self-interest, but merely consideration for the time and efforts of others.

And after the shower is over, the bridesmaid can help her friend in yet another way—addressing and stamping all those thank-you notes!

• Rehearsing for Tomorrow •

*C*ustomarily held on the day before the wedding, the rehearsal has a tendency to become an oddly serious occasion, when somber emotions seem to prevail and prewedding jitters get hold of just about everyone. It is at this time that the bridal attendant can provide much needed help—reining in excited youngsters, clarifying clergy's instructions, reassuring all with her poise and confidence. Later, spirits are revived at the rehearsal dinner, generally hosted by the groom's family. This is the traditional time for the bride and bridegroom to give their special gifts to the bridal party.

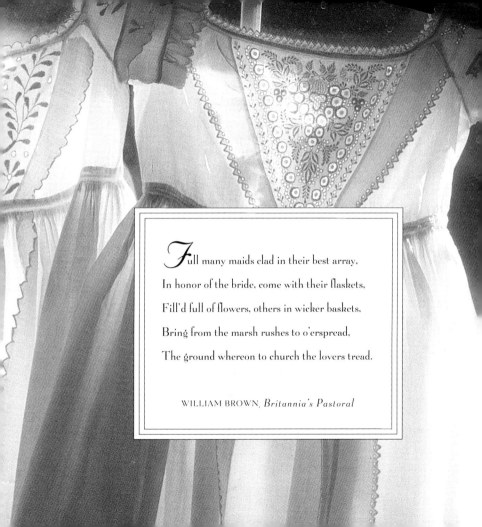

Full many maids clad in their best array,

In honor of the bride, come with their flaskets,

Fill'd full of flowers, others in wicker baskets,

Bring from the marsh rushes to o'erspread,

The ground whereon to church the lovers tread.

WILLIAM BROWN, *Britannia's Pastoral*

• Magical Flowers •

$\mathcal{T}$he tradition of flowers at weddings is as old as the wedding rite itself. Two thousand years ago, Greek and Roman brides would walk toward an altar wearing garlands of herbs and flowers that symbolized innocence. Young girls—themselves symbols of fertility— proceded the brides carrying sheaves of wheat to represent the fruitfulness of the harvest and the hope of a large family for the bride and groom. Centuries later, Elizabethan brides clutched charming nosegays of herbs and wild flowers dotted with greens such as ivy and myrtle to symbolize the deep roots of marriage. Chives, garlic, yarrow, Queen Anne's lace, bachelor buttons, daisies, and marjoram all had significance for the bride. Some warded off evil spirits. Others were thought to be aids to love and faithfulness. Rosemary was the most beloved herb of all, immortalized for lovers by William Shakespeare's declaration, "There's rosemary, for remembrance."

As vegetable gardens began to make way for cultivated flowers, herbs were replaced in nosegays by flowers we find familiar today: roses, pansies, marigolds, violets, dianthus, lilies, and baby's breath. In a generous new custom, the bride and her bridesmaids would fashion tiny nosegays as favors for all the wedding guests. And just before the wedding, bridesmaids would knot fresh flowers into yards of rope for decorating the wedding celebration.

The Victorians turned the nosegay into the larger tussie-mussie, a floral design still dearly loved today. A versatile clutch of flowers surrounded by a lace or filigree ruff and hung with satin streamers, the tussie-mussie was as popular for the bridesmaid as it was for the bride.

Early in the 1800s the bridesmaid was opulently arrayed with her own headdress and veil, often braided with exotic hothouse flowers such as

lilies, stephanotis, and orange blossoms. Rosebud garlands are still worn by bridal attendants as a sign of an unspoiled spirit.

After the wedding, a thoughtful and imaginative bridesmaid might press or preserve any flowers that have survived this emotional day. A delicate dried arrangement or a few blooms in a silver frame makes a very personal gift for a bride returning from her wedding trip.

• In the Looking Glass •

$\mathcal{M}$ ost weddings are at least a few hours long, and some last all day and all night, but all encompass a broad spectrum of emotions and responsibilities for which the bridal attendant must prepare. Anticipating contingencies, yet keeping her eye on the main event, the bridesmaid readies. Comfortable pumps or satin slippers, already "broken in," will lift her over trails of rose petals, hold her aloft through sentimental dances. Her dress, pressed and ready, waits until the last minute. Her hairstyle, pretested and approved, will look beguiling in church light and candlelight—not to mention wedding album photographs afterward. White gloves and a small charming purse add a touch of finesse to an already exquisite outfit.

In days past, part of the bridal attendant's duties at the ceremony was to hold scent bottles in case the bride was overcome with emotion. Taking along a supply of tissues or handkerchieves might be today's version of that custom. Traditionally, before leaving for the ceremony, the bridesmaid inspects the flowers for the bridal party, removing any wilted petals or carelessly left-behind thorns. She makes certain all corsages have extra pins and tucks spare combs and hairpins in a box with the floral headdresses.

Many Victorian weddings featured fans with flowers as bouquets carried by bridal attendants. If the wedding day promises to be warm, this quaint custom might be revived. Providing fans for guests is a thoughtful gesture. Inscribed with the name of the bride and groom in an elegant calligraphic hand, these make memorable wedding favors. If summer showers look imminent, paper parasols are much more festive than nylon umbrellas, and they, too, can be kept as mementos.

• The Wedding Day •

*T*hough it has long been a custom for members of the bridal party to stay with the bride the night before the wedding so they can begin to prepare for the festivities early the next morning, this is not always done in the face of today's changed living arrangements. That is unfortunate, as the night together with good friends can turn into a revelry of high spirits and nostalgia. But whenever the bridal attendants assemble can be an occasion to celebrate. Everyone should be

alert and in good cheer, hiding any nerves, which can be contagious. Bridesmaids should arrange beforehand to have hot steaming coffee, freshly baked muffins or croissants, and fruit salad ready to lift the burden of breakfast from a distracted bride. If there is one day when considerate gestures speak volumes, it is the wedding day.

In almost every culture the bride is prepared by female friends or family members for her wedding in a ritual dressing ceremony. Some can be elaborate and hours long, such as those still done today in most Asian countries. In this country, the bride's dressing has become a photography session. If the wedding is being recorded, members of the bridal party might want to make provisions for this, adjusting makeup to look as good under camera lights as it does in daylight and allowing extra time for photo setups.

"Something old, something new, something borrowed, something blue . . . and a silver sixpence in her shoe." As whimsical as it may seem, this practice is still carefully observed by many brides. Why fly in the face of tradition? With its origins lost in the mists of time, the "old and new" is

thought by many wedding historians to symbolize life and love itself. "Something borrowed" from a happily married woman may bring good luck to the bride. "Something blue" is thought to represent the purity of spirit in some religions, "and a silver sixpence in her shoe" is every sensible woman's goal of starting out her marriage journey with a little wealth just for herself. Today, some brides still observe the tradition of the garter, worn really only to be thrown at unmarried male guests.

After putting on her gown, the bride usually requires the bridesmaid's assistance with her headdress, crown, or garland. If a veil is attached to the headdress, the bridal attendant will help arrange it in a graceful flow. Most likely, the bride and her bridesmaids will have already considered every detail of the bridal ensemble; they will have tried out various hairstyles and will know how to handle the flowers, veil, and more.

Certainly, being a troubleshooter falls within the bridesmaid's job description. Packing a pretty floral bag or a lace-lined straw basket with emergency supplies would be a wonderful security blanket for everyone in the

wedding party: needle and thread, dental floss, combs, a variety of safety pins, hair spray, breath spray, spot remover, aspirin, and, as a treat, a box of chocolate-covered mints. If a double-ring ceremony is planned, the bride may ask the maid of honor to hold the ring she will give the groom until the ceremony. It should of course be kept in a safe and accessible place, perhaps tied around the wrist with a piece of picot-edged satin ribbon or zipped into a small purse.

As it comes time to leave for the ceremony, the bridesmaids help the bride into her car, arranging her gown, train, and veil so that they will resist wrinkles. At the church, as the first musical notes swell through the air, the bridal attendants gather together. The bride, her veil arranged in a heavenly array, is the last to leave, and, for the moment, all is perfect.

• Witness to the Future •

$\mathcal{S}$igning the bridal register is an old and honored custom. For centuries, two witnesses have been required to make a marriage valid, first in church law, later in state law. This was done in order to determine that the marriage was voluntary on both sides and that the bride and groom were indeed the people they represented themselves to be. In many European countries, the signing takes place after the vows as a major element of the ceremony itself. In this country, it can be done either before the ceremony or after.

$\mathcal{G}$od, the best maker of all marriages,

combine your hearts in one.

WILLIAM SHAKESPEARE

• A Celebration of Love •

*A*fter all the preparation and work, the wedding ceremony is over, and your friend is a bride. This is a moment to savor. Standing next to the groom in the receiving line, the maid of honor acts as part hostess, part celebrity. Every guest is glad to see her, lavishing deserved praise on her appearance. She knows many personally and can greet them with warmth and affection. Next to the bride, the other members of the bridal party add their greetings as guests make their way to a wonderful celebration. There will certainly be toasts to the new couple, and though this has traditionally been the provenance of the best man, it is a charming new

custom to call upon the maid of honor or another bridal attendant to add her voice to the wishes for the couple. Simple words, softly spoken, are more eloquent now than the fanciest phrases—perhaps an anecdote that illuminates what she finds so dear about her friend. Reading from a poem or prayer that captures the sentiments of the day is always moving.

At the bridal table, the bridesmaid has a unique perspective on her friend's new world, and with grace and affection can help both sides of this extended family understand and enjoy one another's heritage and traditions.

Before long, the bride prepares to depart for her honeymoon. Once again, a member of the bridal party can be of invaluable help. The bridal gown should be inspected for any damage needing repair before it is

packed away. This task usually falls to the maid of honor or a bridesmaid.

And then it's time for one last bridal tradition—tossing the bridal bouquet. Because it can be heartbreaking to part with it, many brides have a second bouquet created so they can preserve their own bouquet for a keepsake. In the past, some brides composed their wedding bouquets of a score of little bouquets, separating them after the wedding and giving one to each attendant. This would be a lovely custom to revive, as it ensures that each bridesmaid will share in the bride's good fortune.

With the keen eyes, strong arms, and determination of major league outfielders, the crowd gathers and prepares for the bridal toss. Up, up the bouquet soars—and if a lucky bridesmaid should catch it, this could be a little more than a charming coincidence. But we won't tell!

• A Tradition Continues •

*P*ractically every child knows "three times a bridesmaid, never a bride." But do they know "seven times a bridesmaid" guarantees a happy marriage for one so popular? In the past, young women vied to be included in their friends' weddings. Knowing that as bridesmaids they would dress up in beautiful clothes and attract the attention of eligible bachelors gave the role an added dimension. Even though women's roles have changed today, and marriage is no longer the sole measure of happiness and success, to be a bridesmaid and share in the glory of a friend is still a true act of love and an abiding example of the bond of friendship between women.

$\mathcal{G}$irls, close the doors now. Our part is over.

And you, happy pair, God bless you.

CATULLUS

A Lovely Memory

A Bridesmaid's Keepsake Journal

Oh, better than the minting

Of a gold-crowned King

Is the safe-kept memory

Of a lovely thing.

SARA TEASDALE

....

Wedding Date

....

Time   Place

....

The Bride   The Groom

·The Wedding Party·

....

....

....

....

....

....

....

....

· Special Guests ·

Family   *Friends*

....

....

....

....

....

....

....

Love is, above all, the gift of oneself.

JEAN ANOUILH

· When my friend asked me to be a bridesmaid ·

....

....

....

....

· What makes her a dear friend ·

....

....

....

· How we became friends ·

....

....

....

....

....

....

....

....

· Wonderful memories we share ·

....

....

....

....

....

....

....

....

The truth is friendship to me is every bit as sacred and eternal as marriage.

KATHERINE MANSFIELD

· What I have learned from our friendship ·

....

....

....

....

· What I hope for the future ·

....

....

....

· The Bridal Shower ·

Date

Place

....

....

Guests

....

....

....

....

....

....

....

....

....

....

· Rehearsal Dinner ·

Date

Place

....

Guests

....

....

....

....

....

· Toasts ·

....

....

....

....

· The bride's gift to me ·

....

....

....

The Bridesmaids' Dresses

· My gown ·

....

....

....

....

· Headdress, jewelry and shoes ·

....

....

....

· Shopping with the bride ·

....

....

....

....

....

· Our favorite shops ·

....

....

My Bouquet

The Bride's Bouquet

· The Ceremony ·

....

....

....

....

....

....

....

....

·Special Moments·

....

....

....

....

....

....

....

....

· The Reception ·

....

....

....

....

....

....

....

....

The Menu

....

....

....

....

....

....

....

· The Toast ·

....

....

....

....

· Who caught the bouquet ·

....

....

....

· My wishes for the bride and groom ·

....

....

....

....

....

....

....

....

· My gift to the new couple ·

....

....

....

....

....

....

....

....

Good bye," said the fox. "And now here is my secret, a very simple secret: it is only with the heart that one can see rightly; what is essential is invisible to the eye..."

ANTOINE DE SAINT-EXUPÉRY
THE LITTLE PRINCE

Art Credits

Bridesmaids Dinner, April 25, 1905, Given By Eben Wright: 26; courtesy of Museum of The City of New York, The Byron Collection. Winslow Homer, *Two Ladies*: 10; courtesy of The Metropolitan Museum of Art, Gift of Estate of Florence Baird Meyer, in her memory, 1918 (18.123.3). Edmund Blair Leighton, *Signing the Register*: 52; courtesy of City of Bristol Museum & Art Gallery. Photograph, June 20, 1915: 6; courtesy of The New York Public Library Picture Collection. Photograph: 37; courtesy of The New York Public Library Picture Collection. Photographs by Wendi Schneider: 4, 28, 38, 39, 51, 55. Photographs by Maria Taglienti: 3, 9, 12, 16, 19, 21, 23, 24, 30, 32, 36, 40, 43, 44, 49, 59, 61, 64.

ISBN: 0-8362-8053-9

Printed in Singapore
First U.S. edition

1   3   5   7   9   10   8   6   4   2

Text by Arlene Hamilton Stewart
Edited by Laurie Orseck
Designed by Nina Ovryn
Produced by Smallwood and Stewart, Inc.,
New York City

Credits and copyright notices appear on page 95